CW00538324

POLLOCK THE EARLY YEARS

1935-1972

Frank Richardson

ACKNOWLEDGEMENTS

I would like to thank the following people in the preparation for this book. Retired drivers Bob Lumsden, Wullie Sked, Tam Liddle and mechanic Bobby Vass for their long term memories, Bob Erskine and John Henderson for their help with photographs, all the Pollock family for their assistance. Ex Pollock driver Tam Marshall for his help in names and places and finally to my wife Carol for all the typing which included many alterations and corrections.

Published by FRANK RICHARDSON

Copyright
FRANK RICHARDSON

No. 11 NIGHT SCOTSMAN

Front Cover: This 1963 Atkinson eight wheeler was overhauled and repainted in 1968. Driver Davy Auld is standing in front of the vehicle in the summer of 1968 and is on his way north on the A1 heading for the Musselburgh depot.

(photo Frank Richardson)

Apart from pictures taken by the author every effort has been made to trace original photographers but stand corrected if wrongly credited.

CONTENTS

DEDICATION

I've dedicated this book to my friend from childhood, Martin Faulds.   We both had a lifelong interest in transport and living beside the A1 we had a daily opportunity to watch it.   His knowledge of transport was enormous but as far a he was concerned, there was only one haulage company, POLLOCK.   This picture of Martin standing beside No 26 Albion Reiver JSY 789 was taken just outside Cockburnspath Hotel in the early 60's.   He is a lot slimmer here than most people remember him.   Sadly Martin died at the relatively early age of 57 years and his jovial company is sadly missed.   This Midlothian registered Albion was one of the vehicles which joined the fleet when the transport side of Dalkeith Transport was taken over in 1963.

One particular morning in the 1970's after Martin had spent the night with me on night shift where I worked in an Edinburgh hospital, we went along to Leith to have a couple of pints in The Cavern in Constitution Street.   Finishing at 6am the pub didn't open until 7am.   We had a wee while to wait and sat in the car beside the Water of Leith until opening time.   From somewhere in the streets behind us came the sound of a lorry as it pulled away from a standstill.   Martin listened and forwarded "Atkinson Borderer, Gardner 180, Moffat of Cardenden hauling for Jet".   Round the corner came exactly what he had said.

MARTIN FAULDS

1946 - 2004

INTRODUCTION

Growing up as a young boy in the 1950's and 60's I lived in the small village of Cockburnspath, locally known as Copath in Berwickshire in southern Scotland. Located on the A1 at the bottom of a steep hill it was a great place to watch the passing road traffic. I've always been fascinated by any form of transport be it ship, aircraft or road based, but my soft spot was always for lorries. The large numbers of Scottish fleets were usually painted to a high standard and when I got my first camera I had a ready subject.

Many Scottish firms such as Tripney of Grangemouth, Russell of Bathgate, Charles Alexander & Partners, Saddlers of Edinburgh, Dobson of Edinburgh, Allisons of Dundee plus numerous smaller firms have all gone. Pollock on the other hand has survived and prospered.   After photographing their vehicles for some months, some of the drivers would stop and I was able to get better shots. Gradually I got to know most of the drivers and travelled up and down the A1 with them. Visiting the Musselburgh yard on a Saturday morning with a friend, we would be treated to tea and egg rolls courtesy of Ian Pollock.   It would have been all to easy for drivers to dismiss the likes of myself as a young boy but I always found Pollock's drivers to uphold the best qualities in Scottish men, such as friendliness and going out of their way to help people.   Many of the older drivers who are seen throughout the book such as Alec Fairbairn, Charlie Waugh, Bob Cowe, Tam Liddle and Jock Wilson I counted as personal friends.

Finally, I don't think a book such as this could be written at the present time. Various issues such as vehicle parking, Health and Safety and security of haulage yards would limit the freedom I enjoyed during the 1960's to obtain these photographs.   Another problem which could arise would be taking pictures of people at their work which can infringe their privacy.   As can be seen from the pictures throughout the book all the drivers enjoyed having their picture taken and were very proud to stand beside their vehicles.

Frank Richardson   2008

BRIEF HISTORY OF THE FIRM

Prior to establishing his transport business Mr William George Dunn Pollock started his working life as a joiner and served his time with a joinery business in Gorgie, Edinburgh. His interest always lay in transport and the family recall an incident when he was working on a roof as a joiner and struck his thumb with a hammer as he was always being distracted by passing lorries. Later on many of his thoughts and ideas on vehicles could be seen to be viewed from a tradesman's eye. His sons' George and Ian also recalls an involvement in threshing machinery early in his working life. His first driving and haulage experience was with a firm called Davidson who were based in Stevenson Road, Gorgie. When he set up on his own in 1935 he moved to North Gyle Farm in Corstorphine where he rented sheds. The next move was to Gylemuir Road, Corstorphine where he remained until nationalization in 1949. Another short lived business interest was the running of two Maudsley Coaches, one painted green and the other in Pollock livery. Always on the look out for licences he took over the business of Daniel Forrest at Braehead in Lanarkshire about 1947. With impending nationalization the family related firm of Pettigrew of Corstorphine decided to give up general haulage and transferred six vehicles to Pollock. Some of Pettigrew's work was the movement of stage props between theatres which Pollock did not continue with. Pollock gradually grew larger, but in 1949 their fleet was nationalized. During nationalization he became a Group Manager with British Road Services and was responsible for the East Lothian and Borders division based at the Haddington depot. This comprised approximately 230 vehicles spread over 11 depots.

When De-Nationalization of Road Transport came in 1954 he bought back vehicles from British Road Services. He set up haulage operations at 101 Newbigging, Musselburgh as Pollock (Musselburgh) Ltd and remained there through the 60's and 70's until 1981 when they shifted about a mile away to Olivebank on the west side of Musselburgh. During the 60's, WGD Pollock was assisted by his sons, George who looked after administration and Ian who looked after the traffic side. The first depot outside Musselburgh was opened in Stebondale Street, London E14 and this was used by day trunkers, but night trunk services used Express Carriers depot in Nelson Street, Stepney. This had a tight entrance and artics had to swing across Nelson Street and reverse in. This company was formed in 1945 by well known haulage firms in Scotland namely Pollock, Munro's of Aberdeen, Russell of Bathgate and Dalkeith Transport and Storage. Eventually the company would be wholly owned by Pollock. About 1964 a west coast night trunk was started running to and from Birmingham with south bound loads being mainly from Colville's steel to the factories in the Midlands. This depot was in Pensnett Estate at Kingswinford. Paper from the many surrounding mills such as Inveresk in Musselburgh, Galloways of Balerno and Cowans of Penicuik made up many a Pollock load. In 1963 the haulage side of the business of Dalkeith Transport and Storage was acquired and this added 23 vehicles to the fleet. They hauled paper from Todds Mill in Lasswade and Todds Mill in Polton. In November 1969 Walkers of Leith (ALEXANDER C WALKER) were taken over. This was a small concern with only three vehicles. Two Albion Clydesdale Ergomatic cab four wheelers were kept and repainted into the fleet colours but the Leyland Comet LAD Artic was disposed of. The Comet's regular run was to take castings from a company called Boncast at Primrose Works in Jane Street, Leith down to Sheffield. It went over to Nantwich where it picked up a load of moulding sand for the return trip north. The early 60's vehicles such as the Leyland Octopuses and AEC Marshals carried small names in script form but it was with the coming of the Atkinson in 1962 that the naming and tartan really got under way. Many of the touches such as fairy lights on top of the cab came from WGD's frequent visits to North America. Some of the vehicles such as the Albion Reivers of which there were quite a few never carried a name or tartan. The end of the 60's saw the introduction of foreign vehicles such as Scania and later Volvo to the fleet and this trend would continue to the present day. In 1971 Pollock (Musselbugh) Ltd was sold to Hilton Transport Services (HTS) for £260,400 but retained the right to keep their vehicles in the same colours. Father George and sons Ian and George continued to run the business after the takeover and were in a position to retake control in 1975 when the Hilton Group went into receivership. The beginning of the 1970's brings to an end the period covered by this book.

POLLOCK FLEET AND DRIVERS IN 1958

LEYLAND BEAVER 4 WHL	WULLIE SKED
LEYLAND BEAVER 4 WHL	T. RENWICK
LEYLAND BEAVER 4 WHL	S. STUART
LEYLAND BEAVER 4 WHL	TAM LIDDLE
E R F 4 WHL	TAM TURNER
A E C MERCURY 4 WHL	T. TAYLOR
A E C MERCURY 4 WHL	J. CULLEN
LEYLAND SUPER COMET 4 WHL	R. TURNER
LEYLAND COMET 4 WHL	GEORDIE DUNN
LEYLAND COMET 4 WHL	ALEC FAIRBAIRN
B M C 4 WHL	BILLY MITCHELL
LEYLAND COMET 6 WHL	TAM CRAMB
LEYLAND STEER 6 WHL	JOCK WILSON
LEYLAND STEER 6 WHL	J. REID
LEYLAND STEER 6 WHL	JOCK DOIG
LEYLAND STEER 6 WHL	TAM RAYNOR
ERF 6 WHL	MATTY KENNEDY
LEYLAND OCTOPUS 8 WHL	DICK MURRAY
A E C MAMMOTH MAJOR 8 WHL	GEORGE LOGAN

SHUNTERS	JIMMY MITCHELL & T. CRAMB SEN.
MECHANIC	PETER DUNCAN

Information as supplied by T. Liddle when he first joined Pollock.

5

The founder WGD Pollock in his office at Gylemuir Road, Edinburgh

EARLY YEARS

WGD Pollock was a frequent visitor to Canada and is pictured here on the right beside his wife, mother and father and sister Flo. This particular visit saw them travel to Winnipeg in the 1930's travelling out on the Cunard steamship *CARONIA*. His uncle had emigrated some years previous and had built three blocks of apartments Locarno, Willingdon and the Pollock apartments in Winnipeg. The temptation to stay in Canada must have been attractive as he had quite a few relations established there. His mother and father were farmers who farmed at Baberton Farm to the west of Edinburgh. WGD also had a farming interest in his early years and ran two travelling threshing mills.

BEDFORD

Left: This Bedford is reputedly the first vehicle owned by William Pollock when he set up his business in Edinburgh in 1935. Loads were bags of grain to the flour mills in Fife such as Hutchison in Kirkaldy.

(photo Pollock Collection)

CORSTORPHINE

Right: The founder WGD Pollock stands beside a line up at the Gylemuir Road, Corstorphine yard in the west of Edinburgh. The ERF he is standing beside has the name FORTH below the side window which indicates the Daniel Forrest connection. Although his name appeared on the lorries as William Pollock he was generally known in business and to friends and family as George.

(photo Pollock Collection)

No. 4 LEYLAND BEAVER   VD 8978

Left: Pollock has always acquired companies over the years and one of the earliest was Daniel Forrest from Braehead near Forth in Lanarkshire.   The four wheel Leyland photographed here about 1935 with the livestock transporter body is standing at a farm and there are some similarities in the livery and lettering layout to the early Pollock vehicles.

(photo courtesy John Tennant Collection)

LEYLAND CUB

Right: The load on this Daniel Forrest four wheel Leyland Cub looks like potatoes when this photograph was taken in the 1930's. The regular work for this company was livestock and milk and the livery was mainly dark green. The young lad in the dust coat looks more like a dairyman rather than a farm worker.

According to Forrest driver Jim Reid when Pollock took over Forrest about 1947 their fleet comprised six vehicles, a long nosed Bedford, two Leyland Cubs, two Leyland Beavers and a Leyland Lion bus chassis with a platform body.

(photo courtesy John Tennant Collection)

No. 7 LEYLAND STEER   *Above:*   This brand new Leyland Steer photographed in Edinburgh had Pollock's colours but Dan Forrest's name. After the takeover of Dan Forrest about 1947 Pollock sent down replacement vehicles such as this Steer along with a Vulcan, Albion Chieftain, Maudsley Mogul and a long nosed Commer.   Supplied and fitted out by Joseph Wilkinson (Motors) Ltd, Hope Crescent, Edinburgh

(photo J. Campbell Harper / Joseph Wilkinson Motors Ltd)

VULCAN

Left: One of the small four wheel Vulcan lorries which formed part of the fleet when the firm was based at Corstorphine in Edinburgh. The Vulcan is pictured here parked in Angle Park Terrace in Gorgie beside the showroom of the motor agents H C Hutchison, and the 'G' in the number plate would date this vehicle to 1947-1948.

(photo Pollock Collection)

No.11 ERF

Right: This six wheel ERF No. 11 in the fleet illustrates the earlier style of lettering and this photo would have been taken when the base was in Corstorphine, Edinburgh. Date of the vehicle approximately 1947.

(photo Pollock Collection)

No. 15 LEYLAND STEER

Left: This Arthur Ingram shot was taken at the entrance to the Nelson Street Depot in Stepney in 1958. It is parked just forward of the fuel point with its nose heading out of the yard towards Nelson Street.

(photo Arthur Ingram / Roundoak Publishing)

No. 18 ERF

Right: This British Road Service eight wheel ERF has the Pollock connection shown on the side raves above the rear wheels. This vehicle has the "Streamline" cab and the style of the side lights would date it to the early 50's.

(photo Pollock Collection)

No. 10 ERF

Above: This photo was taken at the Nelson Street, Stepney, London Depot by Arthur Ingram in 1958.   Its Roxburghshire registration would suggest that it was one of the vehicles bought after de-nationalization of road transport in 1954.

(photo Arthur Ingram / Roundoak Publishing)

No. 16 LEYLAND BEAVER

Above: This four wheel Leyland Beaver has a Fife registration and driver Tam Liddle drove it in the late 1950's. It came from a fruit and vegetable company called Crawford who were based near Dunfermline possibly at Crossgates. Photographed here in 1958 at Stepney, London.

(photo Arthur Ingram / Roundoak Publishing)

No. 6 LEYLAND STEER
Above: This Berwickshire registered Leyland was photographed at Stepney, London by Arthur Ingram in 1958.   Its regular driver at this time was Tam Raynor.

(photo Arthur Ingram / Roundoak Publishing)

6

AEC

AEC MERCURY

Left: This photo is thought to have been taken in London. Its driver at this time in the 1950's was Tam Taylor and the vehicle was new in 1954.

(photo Roger Kenney)

No. 20 FLYING SCOTSMAN

Right: A rather grubby and battered looking "FLYING SCOTSMAN" stands in the yard at Musselburgh. The load is empty casks for the whisky industry. According to driver Tam Liddle these casks were known as A.S.B.'s (American Spirit Barrels). He remembers the AEC as being very slow and put it down to it only having a 5 speed gearbox, although on the plus side it had power steering and also had flashing indicators. Its maximum speed was 43-44mph. This was quite a bit slower when compared to the Albion Reivers in the fleet which could do 50-55mph. These casks were used by the whisky industry for storage and conditioning.

(photo Frank Richardson)

No. 5 THE CLANSMAN

Left: This AEC Marshal is standing outside the yard at 101, Newbigging and recently had a full cab repaint. Its six speed gearbox gave a much improved performance compared with the earlier Marshal YSC 888 with the five speed gearbox. Behind the Marshal is the Cummins 220 powered Atkinson, "OVERLANDER" and to the right is AEC Mercury "VIRGINIAN" with a single axle Crane Freuhauf box van.

(photo Frank Richardson)

No. 16 THE TALISMAN

Right: Driver Tam Crawford brings "THE TALISMAN" to a halt on the A1 in Berwickshire as it heads back up north to the Musselburgh yard. These AEC Marshals had the tartan on the door flashes as well as the front grills, in this case Buchanan tartan.

(photo Frank Richardson)

No. 50 SCOTIA'S PRIDE
Left: One of a pair of AEC Mandators new in 1964 "SCOTIA'S PRIDE" is coming up the old Haddington by-pass on the old A1. This vehicle had a short life with Pollock, being disposed of in 1967.

(photo Frank Richardson)

No. 43 ROB ROY
Below Left: Pollock's trailer fleet was almost 100% Crane Fruehauf but in this shot "ROB ROY" is pulling a York tandem axle trailer with the open diamonds on the frames.

(photo Frank Richardson)

No. 1 STINGRAY
Below: This 1964 AEC Mercury tractor had a short life with Pollock lasting only two years before being sold on. Seen here in April 1965.

(photo Joe Donaldson)

No. 34 APACHE

Above: Pollock was one of the few operators who ran AEC Mercury tractors with double axle semi-trailers. With a large load "APACHE" slows for traffic lights at Cockburnspath heading north on the A1 towards Musselburgh. Cockburnspath Hotel in the background closed shortly after a new bypass was built leaving the village without a pub. "APACHE" new in 1964 was sold in 1969 to a west of Scotland haulage contractor Houston and repainted green.

(photo Frank Richardson)

No. 39 CRUSADER
Above: Parked outside the Musselburgh garage after a complete repaint. The Mercury by this time was engaged on local work.

(photo Frank Richardson)

No. 37 SUNDOWNER

Left: This was the last pre-Ergomatic cab AEC Mercury tractor to be supplied to Pollock before the introduction of the Ergomatic cab Mercurys. They covered large distances being used all over the country.

(photo Frank Richardson)

No. 26 SCOTIA'S PRIDE & No. 12 GLOBE TROTTER

Right: The low winter sun shines on "SCOTIA'S PRIDE" and "GLOBE TROTTER" in December 1968. At this time of the year the daylight in southern Scotland starts to fade about half past three in the afternoon. Tam Liddle, the driver of the Marshal was responsible for fitting the chrome wheel embellishers.

(photo Frank Richardson)

No. 1 DAY TRIPPER
Above: Bert Todd has reversed "DAY TRIPPER" into the Kenning tyre depot in Chesterfield, and with the van doors open the unloading has started tyre by tyre.

(photo Frank Richardson)

No. 41 MOONSPINNER   *Above:*   One of the first of the Ergomatic cab AEC Mercurys, "MOONSPINNER"   passes the village of Cockburnspath heading south on the A1.   Taken in August 1966 the Mercury would be almost brand new.   Behind the village looking north the North Sea can be seen. The "MOON-SPINNERS"   was a 1964 film starring Hayley Mills and involved a jewel theft set in Crete.

(photo Frank Richardson)

No.1 DAY TRIPPER

Above: Named after the Beatles hit record this 1964 AEC Ergomatic cab Mercury "DAY TRIPPER" replaced the earlier AEC Mercury "STINGRAY" as No. 1 in the fleet.   Seen here coupled to a single axle Crane Fruehauf van.

(photo Frank Richardson)

No. 26 SCOTIA'S PRIDE

Left: This shot of the AEC Marshal shows the length of the 27 feet long platform and one of the 75 gallon fuel tanks.   With two 75 gallon tanks the range was 1200 miles from fill up.   They were very economical sometimes returning 10 miles per gallon.   The platform on these Marshals was actually 3 feet longer than the 24 feet platforms fitted to the Atkinson eight wheelers.   When bringing barley back up north from Cambridge the Marshals were loaded with a hundred bags as against the Atkinsons with ninety five bags.   Its first driver Tam Liddle remembers this vehicle with affection and cannot think of having had much trouble with it.

(photo Frank Richardson)

No. 16 LIVELY LADY

Right: Named after the yacht "LIVELY LADY" which was sailed round the world single handed by Sir Alec Rose.   Geordie Wright arrives in the Musselburgh yard with "LIVELY LADY" clean and shining with chrome bumper.   Geordie's previous driving career had been with a two vehicle firm called William Watt and run by Jimmy Alves.   Jimmy drove an AEC Mercury and Geordie had a LAD cab Albion Reiver.

(photo Frank Richardson)

No. 28 DAKTARI *Above:* Heading south on the A1 "DAKTARI" sits on the Royal Borders Bridge at Berwick-upon-Tweed on a Saturday morning in January 1968.   It's a fairly quiet scene considering all A1 traffic had to pass through Berwick as the bypass didn't exist at this time. "DAKTARI" was produced by Corgi to celebrate Pollock's seventy years in business.   Alec Fairbairn, one of Pollock's gentleman drivers, seen here drove the AEC from new having previously driven the Atkinson eight wheeler "PONDEROSA" 7081 SC.

(photo Frank Richardson)

No.40 VIRGINIAN

Above: With a light covering of snow on the ground Wattie Howden couples up "VIRGINIAN", a brand new AEC Ergomatic cab Mercury to a Crane Fruehauf van. Regular loads for this van were carpets from Widnells Factory in Bonnyrigg, Midlothian.

(photo Frank Richardson)

No. 46 TRIDENT II

Left: Replacing the Leyland Comet in 1968, "TRIDENT II" was the first of four Ergomatic cab AEC Mercury flatbed 16 tonners. Bodywork by Kirkness and Innes, Eskbank, Nr Dalkeith, it stands empty in the Musselburgh yard on a Saturday morning. These AEC Mercurys were frequently used on long distance work.

(photo Frank Richardson)

No. 42 EAGLE

Below Left: One of the 1969 four wheel AEC Mercury flatbeds is negotiating the streets past Milnes Cold Store. The platform on these vehicles was 24 feet long, the same length as the Atkinson eight wheelers.

(photo Joe Donaldson)

No. 45 COLUMBIA

Below: This four wheel AEC Mercury is standing in Leith with a 20 feet container tied on with rope. This was common practise before the advent of twistlocks. It suffered severe damage in an accident on the A68, but because it wasn't very old it was straightened and a new cab fitted. On the right is a Leyland Comet belonging to the papermakers Galloways of Balerno.

(photo Joe Donaldson)

7

ATKINSON
TRACTORS

No.49 DAKOTAS

Left: Chapelhill at Cockburnspath, Berwickshire was one of the steeper gradients on the A1 heading south and reduced many lorries to a crawl. "DAKOTAS" here is about halfway up the hill and is being driven by Bert Todd. The chrome plated panther adornment on the radiator was known as Aitkens Panther.

(photo Frank Richardson)

No. 7 BURKE'S LAW

Right: Travelling south on the A1 at Chapelhill, Cockburnspath, "BURKE'S LAW" has the classic Pollock load, low with the extra sitting on top of the tandem axles.

(photo Frank Richardson)

No. 6 GOLDFINGER
Above: Drivers Jimmy Watson and Davy Auld enjoy a break on a warm sunny day in June 1968. The four orange fairy lights can be seen above the Pollock headboard and were an easy way of recognising a Pollock vehicle at night.
(photo Frank Richardson)

No.15 FUGITIVE

Left: "FUGITIVE" has just pulled into the Musselburgh yard after returning from the south. Regular driver at this time was Tel Turner.

(photo Frank Richardson)

No. 10 SHANGRI'LA

Below: The regular driver of this Atkinson was Wullie Grandison who washed his vehicles so much the paint literally wore away. The "SHANGRI'LA" name on the Clan Chatton tartan sash has disappeared. In winter many Atkinson drivers blanked off part of the radiator with paper or in this case, part of a cardboard carton, because the Gardner 150 engine ran very cool.

(photo Frank Richardson)

No. 32 HIGHLAND WEDDING

Opposite Page: Impressive Rolls Royce powered six wheel Atkinson tractor with a load of steel from Gartcosh. "HIGHLAND WEDDING" was named after a horse which won the 1968 Grand National. When worked hard hauling heavy loads uphill the Rolls Royce engines are remembered for having a very smoky exhaust. Photo taken on the A1 about a month after delivery to Pollocks. The driver standing beside it is Jimmy Watson.

(photo Frank Richardson)

No. 19 OVERLANDER

Left: Powered by the Cummins 220 engine, "OVERLANDER" leads the ERF of John Russell (Grangemouth) Ltd which has the smaller Cummins 180 heading south on the A1. Matty Kennedy was given this tractor when new in 1966 and it was remembered as a fast machine, 80 mph being possible. Also very hard on brakes requiring new linings every 6000 - 8000 miles. The noise inside the cab from the 220 engine when running was deafening. There were tyre problems on the rear axle of this trailer because of uneven weight distribution, but this was eventually solved by fitting packers to the first and second axles.

(photo Frank Richardson)

No. 9 UNTOUCHABLE

Right: Not the regular driver of "UNTOUCHABLE" Geordie Menzies always keen for a photograph jumps into the cab when this vehicle was brand new. Taken in January 1968 with a Freightliner container load, this was its first load after delivery. It was fitted with a 220 Rolls Royce diesel engine on a 10ft 6in wheel base chassis.

(photo Frank Richardson)

No. 2 PACEMAKER

Above: Driver Wullie MacCraw stands beside No.2 "PACEMAKER" at Haddington in East Lothian. The farm implement on the back of the trailer is a New Holland Muck Spreader. Photographed on the 20th August 1967.

(photo Frank Richardson)

No. 38 ABLE SCOT

Above: This Cummins powered Atkinson Borderer is standing in a lay-by at the top of Soutra Hill on the A68 on a Sunday morning. Some drivers such as Sandy Watson in the drivers seat here, would leave Musselburgh and head south via the A68 and join the A1 further south. Soutra is a bleak and windy place especially in winter, and is now the site of a large wind farm.

(photo Frank Richardson)

No. 6 GOLDFINGER

Above: Heading south "GOLDFINGER" trundles through the High Street in Dunbar, East Lothian on a Saturday afternoon in the summer of 1966. Compared to the present day running a tri-axle trailer on a Gardner 150 powered unit would seem grossly underpowered.

(photo Frank Richardson)

No. 37 WISE SCOT

Left: This Cummins powered Atkinson tractor with tri-axle trailer is parked up in the Musselburgh yard in the 1970's. Powered by the Cummins 220 engine this was the first Pollock vehicle to travel abroad. It took large cast iron valves from the Glenfield and Kennedy works in Kilmarnock down to Hull and across to Rotterdam on a North Sea Ferry. Bob Erskine was the driver and he delivered them to a shipyard at Krimpen aan De lJsel in the Netherlands.

(photo Frank Richardson)

No. 7 BRAW SCOT

Right: Replacing Atkinson "BURKE'S LAW" as No. 7 in 1972 "BRAW SCOT" a Gardner 240 powered Atkinson has come from Leith and is heading for Musselburgh past Portobello Power Station. The colour of the trailer sheet shows the Hilton Transport Services connection. I served my apprenticeship here as a mechanical fitter during the 1960's and I took this shot from the turbine hall roof. The Power Station was demolished in the 1970's and houses built on the site. This was the second Pollock vehicle to travel abroad from Hull to Rotterdam. Its driver Rab Doig skidded and the Atkinson ended up in a canal. It was recovered and Bob Erskine brought it back to Musselburgh on a low loader. Bob Vass the mechanic drained the Gardner, changed the filters, filled up with oil and it fired up. The cab was rebuilt and the whole vehicle was ready to run three weeks after the accident.

(photo Frank Richardson)

No. 61 FIERY SCOT

Above: This was a Gardner 180 powered Atkinson 6x2 tractor and is heading south on the A1 just south of Grantshouse in Berwickshire. Previously it had been connected to a heavy oil fuel tank driven by Dick Murray. This vehicle is remembered by driver Tam Marshall as having a top speed of only 48 miles per hour. The river in the background of the picture is the Eye Water which gently meanders down to the sea at Eyemouth, and behind the trees lies the main London to Edinburgh railway line.

(photo Frank Richardson)

No. 1 BORDER LASSIE
Left: This Atkinson Borderer has a Berwickshire registration and is seen here in Leith Docks. The trailers to the right are loaded with Holstein Beer crates. KSH 123L has survived into preservation and is now owned by Pollock. (photo Joe Donaldson)

No. 63 SWIFT SCOT
Below Left: One of three Rolls Royce Atkinson tractors "SWIFT SCOT" came up from the London firm George Transport which had been taken over by Hilton Transport Services. Heading back to the Musselburgh yard along Bernard Street in Leith the Atkinson has drawn up at the traffic lights beside the Ford D tipper belonging to John Monteith, Builders from Dalkeith. (photo Joe Donaldson)

No. 9 ROYAL SCOT
Below: Originally painted in the dark blue of Shaws Fuels and carrying fleet No. P65 this Atkinson tractor was painted into Pollock's colours, given the name "ROYAL SCOT" and became fleet No. 9. Seen here standing beside the bonded warehouses in Leith with a load of Whyte & Mackay whisky cartons. (photo Joe Donaldson)

8

ALBION   GUY
& LEYLAND

No. 33 HONEST LASS
Above: One of two Leyland Octupuses with mouth organ cabs which had Midlothian number plates and came from the takeover of the transport side of DalkeithTransport and Storage in 1963.

(photo Joe Donaldson)

No. 32 HONEST LAD
Above Right: This eight wheel Leyland Octopus also came to Pollock from Dalkeith Transport in 1963. By this time Leylands were beginning to lose favour in the fleet.

(photo Pollock Collection)

LEYLAND OCTOPUS
Right: PSC 500 is standing here with the platform empty but sheeted. According to Tam Liddle this was common practice when going to load paper in order to keep the platform dry. Its first driver was Dick Murray. Behind the Octopus is an AEC Mercury with an earlier paintwork style. The cab headboard has the EDINBURGH LONDON and the Pollock Transport name is below the windscreen.

(photo Roger Kenney)

No. 4 ALBION REIVER

Left: The Albion Reiver is leading the AEC Mercury "MOONSPINNER" as they both head home on a Sunday afternoon in 1967. They are crossing over Dunglass Bridge into East Lothian from Berwickshire on the A1 heading north. The AEC Mercury is loaded with ASB's (American Spirit Barrels) for the whisky industry.

(photo Frank Richardson)

No. 21 ALBION REIVER

Right: The Albion Reiver No. 21 crosses the Dunglass Bridge into East Lothian on the A1 in 1966. It's connected to the KV ERF No. 22 by a towbar. All the rigid vehicles carried tow bars. This was common practice coming home, and I always assumed it was because the Reiver was faster than the ERF and the return trip could be completed in a shorter time. Trailing at the back is an AEC Mercury tractor from the BRS Haddington depot.

(photo Frank Richardson)

No. 46 LEYLAND COMET

Left: The small Leyland Comet was new in 1960 and never carried a name or tartan. It's heading here for the waste ground just down the road from the Musselburgh yard. Disposed of in 1968 it was rumoured to have ended up in Ireland. Another subject of a Corgi model in 2005 although featuring the Albion style of the LAD cab rather than the short door version.

(photo Frank Richardson)

No. 9 ALBION REIVER

Right: Albion Reiver No. 9 leads the eight wheeler Atkinson "PONDEROSA" as they head south on the A1 in 1967. Setting of from Musselburgh in the morning a typical day's run would see drivers ending up at the Hilltop, Blyth near Doncaster for an overnight stay.

(photo Frank Richardson)

No.8 ALBION REIVER

Above: One of many ALBION REIVERS in the fleet heading south on the A1 through Berwickshire. When new in 1962 this was one of the Albion exhibits on their stand at the annual motor show held in the Kelvin Hall in Glasgow. This Reiver became the subject of a die cast model from Corgi.

(photo Frank Richardson)

No. 52 MIGHTY QUINN   *Above:*   Named after the Bob Dylan song made famous by Manfred Mann.   This two pedal Leyland Beaver was new in 1968 and was allocated to Andrew Mack.   I photographed it here on the A1 in Berwickshire on its first trip south on Sunday 3rd August 1968.   Its regular load was fondant which was picked up from Fleming-Howden's works at Albert Street in Leith and delivered to bakeries in London such as the large one at Camden Town.   Andrew was an experienced driver having spells as a bus driver and also drove an eight wheel Foden for Lothian Structural Steel before joining Pollock.   Despite its modern appearance the Beaver did not have power steering.

(photo Frank Richardson)

No. 65 WILD SCOT
Left: This Gardner 180 powered Big J came from George Transport, London part of H T S and came along with three Rolls Royce powered Atkinson tractors.   Driver Tam Marshall travelled down to Pollock's depot in Birmingham to bring it back to Musselburgh.   Photographed here on the A1 by the well known Pollock enthusiast Geoff Milne.

(photo Geoff Milne)

No. 56 FAMOUS SCOT
Below Left: This Albion Clydesdale 16 tonner was one of a pair which came from the take over of the small Leith based company Alexander C Walker. These Clydesdales had noticeably shorter platforms compared to the AEC Mercurys.

(photo Joe Donaldson)

No. 55 STAR TREK
Below: This was the other Ergomatic cab Albion Clydesdale 16 tonner which came from the Leith company of Alexander C Walker.

(photo Joe Donaldson)

9

BEDFORD AND BMC

No. 41 FLYING DUTCHMAN

Left: Some of the smaller vehicles in the fleet in the 1960's were Morris four wheelers, and also some of the first to carry names in script form "FLYING DUTCHMAN" standing here in the Musselburgh yard was one of them.

(photo Joe Donaldson)

No. 42 TORNADO

Right: One of the other Morris four wheelers "TORNADO" was unusual in the fleet as it was a tipper.

(photo Joe Donaldson)

No. 44 MORRIS   *Above:* This Morris 4 wheeler was one of the earliest vehicles to carry a tartan sash on its doors (Dress Macleod).   In the yard also are, to the left the AEC Marshal "DAKTARI" and an AEC Mercury tractor to the right.   Pollock vehicles were registered in Edinburgh and would receive number plates with SC, SF, SG, WS and FS.   Dalkeith Transport vehicles were registered in Midlothian and received plates with SY.

(photo Frank Richardson)

No. 39 MORRIS

Left: MORRIS No. 39 stands on waste ground just down the road from the yard in Musselburgh.   The pub in the background is The Bluebell later demolished to make way for housing.   Summer 1967.

(photo Frank Richardson)

No.40 MORRIS

Right: Apart from the elderly ERF C15 these two Morris tractors were the first articulated vehicles to join the Pollock fleet.   Regular work for them was the transport of steel strip components from Bruntons in Musselburgh to the Glacier Bearing Factory in Kilmarnock.   The Morris tractor stands on the waste ground near the Musselburgh yard in the summer of 1965.

(photo Frank Richardson)

No. 42 TRAIL TREKKER

Left: This is a Saturday morning shot taken in the Musselburgh yard at 101, Newbigging.   The Bedford has returned from the local Inveresk paper mill with a load of paper and is in the process of transferring it to make up part of a load for the eight wheeler "DEFENDER" HSF 12E.

(photo Frank Richardson)

No. 45 PATHFINDER

Right: Standing in the entrance to the Musselburgh yard at 101 Newbigging is the TK Bedford "PATHFINDER".   One of a pair of Bedfords bought in 1966.   Used mainly on local work.

(photo Frank Richardson)

10

EIGHT WHEELERS

No. 22 ERF

Above: The eight wheeler ERF's were never noted for their speed and the Morris Minor is actually overtaking going uphill. Ian Baptie heads south at the top of Chapelhill near Cockburnspath with a couple of hitch hikers.

(photo Frank Richardson)

No.11 NIGHT SCOTSMAN   *Above:* Photographed in the north bound lay-by on the A1 to the south of Cockburnspath in June 1968 "NIGHT SCOTSMAN" is on its way back to Musselburgh.   It had recently been overhauled and repainted in March.   The mainly green Colquhoun tartan on the sash stands out well on the red background on the front of the cab.

(photo Frank Richardson)

No.12 GLOBE TROTTER

Above: One of the first of the eight wheel MK1 cab Atkinsons, which eventually numbered eight, "GLOBE TROTTER" heads towards London on the A1 in southern Scotland.   Driven here by Sandy Watson in 1965.

(photo Frank Richardson)

No. 3 TWO CAPITALS
Above: "TWO CAPITALS" waits to turn into the yard at 101 Newbigging, Musselburgh driven by Geordie Wright from Gilmerton, Edinburgh in 1966. Years later 3722 SC was found in a scrap yard by John Douglas from Alston, Cumbria. He bought and restored it and with Pollock's permission painted it into its old colours. (photo Frank Richardson)

No. 32 PONDEROSA
Above: This was one of my favourite looking Pollock vehicles but it came to a terrible end after colliding with a tree in December 1968.
Alec Fairbairn, was its driver at this time and lived near the Union Canal in Edinburgh where I took this shot in 1966.   The vehicle behind is a Commer belonging to Bruce Lindsay, a local coal merchant.

(photo Frank Richardson)

No. 11 NIGHT SCOTSMAN & No.12 GLOBE TROTTER

Above: A young driver from the Currie area and Tam Turner pose beside the first of the Atkinson eight wheelers "GLOBE TROTTER" and "NIGHT SCOTSMAN" when they were both new. The location is on the old A1 beside Musselburgh Race Course.

(photo Pollock Collection)

No. 27 CONCORD
Above: Jock Donaldson gets set to run over and jump into the cab of "CONCORD", one of a pair of eight wheeled Atkinsons delivered new in 1967. Along with No. 33 "DEFENDER" they were the last eight wheeled Atkinsons Pollock ever bought.

(photo Frank Richardson)

No. 33 DEFENDER
Above Right: Jock Wilson has just crossed over the main Edinburgh London East Coast railway line on his way south on the A1. The Atkinson cab on this eight wheeler had slightly wider wheel arches to take account of the spread axles for heavier weights, but it still ran at 24 tons. The North Sea is in the background in this photo taken just to the north of Cockburnspath village in Berwickshire.

(photo Frank Richardson)

No. 32 PONDEROSA
Right: Driver Alec Fairbairn pulls up at Dunglass Bridge on the A1 at the East Lothian - Berwickshire border as he heads back home. This bridge dating from the 1930's is now redundant as a new bridge to the east now carries the A1.

(photo Frank Richardson)

No. 24 TELSTAR

Above: Like many of the vehicle names with a space connection "TELSTAR" was named after a communication satellite which was launched in 1963.
It is seen here standing down the road from the Musselburgh yard entrance on a Saturday morning in 1966. The crossroads behind the eight wheeler
boasted two pubs, The Bluebell and The Horseshoe. The Bluebell on the left hand side was knocked down to make way for housing. Driver at this time
was Davy Scott.

(photo Frank Richardson)

11

ERF

No. 22 KV ERF

Left: Ian Baptie from Haddington was the regular driver of this 1960 KV cab ERF eight wheeler. Photographed in the lay-by south of Cockburnspath, he's heading south on the A1 in 1966.

(photo Frank Richardson)

No. 23 KV ERF

Right: This eight wheel KV cab ERF which was unnamed is going south on the A1 through Berwickshire on a Saturday morning in 1966 driven by Bobby Carr. Two years later in the hands of another driver it went on fire in 1968 in Kent. The cab was badly damaged and was brought back to Scotland on the back of the AEC Marshal "DAKTARI". It was found to be beyond economical repair and was disposed of.

(photo Frank Richardson)

No. 51 THUNDERBIRD

Above: Bob Cowe the driver of "THUNDERBIRD" stayed in Haddington and this photo is taken at the south end of Haddington bypass looking towards East Linton. He is heading home on a Sunday afternoon in December 1967.

(photo Frank Richardson)

No. 18 HAWAIIAN EYE

Left: Empty sherry casks which were destined for the whisky industry made up regular loads from the south. "HAWAIIAN EYE" with Cummins 180 power seen here outside the Eden Hotel in Dunbar, East Lothian in August 1967.

(photo Frank Richardson)

No. 36 BEACHCOMBER

Right: One of three LV ERF tractors, bought in 1964, two with Cummins 180 engines one with Gardner 150. This ERF was driven at this time by Andrew Mack.

(photo Frank Richardson)

No. 18 HAWAIIAN EYE

Left: The queue building up behind the LV cab ERF is quite modest by today's standards but demonstrates the slowing effect on the traffic that Chapelhill had on the A1 in Berwickshire. Even with the Cummins 180 powered engine this hill was still challenging.

(photo Frank Richardson)

No. 18 HAWAIIAN EYE

Right: This photograph shows a typical afternoon on the A1 in the 60's. A lot of Scottish drivers returned home from the south on Sundays and here is Geordie Dunn and ERF No. 18 "HAWAIIAN EYE" pursued by a Scottish and Newcastle brewers KV ERF and No. 33 " DEFENDER" plus one of the Albion Reivers. The location is just north of Grantshouse, Berwickshire and the large wood behind is Penmanshiel Wood. In winter because of the dull daylight in Scotland I used Ilford HP3 film, fast but very grainy.

(photo Frank Richardson)

No. 59 NOBLE SCOT   *Above:*   This attractive ERF tractor was powered by a Gardner 180 engine and driven by one of Pollock's long serving
drivers Tam Raynor.

(photo Joe Donaldson)

12

NIGHT TRUNKS

No. 31 BONANZA

Left: Just about at the top of Chapelhill on the A1 in Berwickshire "BONANZA" pulls the East Coast night trunk trailer heading south to London. Its driver at this time was Charlie Waugh. The passenger side wiper which pivoted from the bottom has been removed. Photographed about 1965.

(photo Frank Richardson)

No. 25 SCARLET O'HARA

Right: This 1963 Atkinson Silver Knight tractor is parked just outside the Musselburgh yard. The other Atkinson at the back is No. 49 "DAKOTAS".

(photo Frank Richardson)

No. 17 AVENGER *Above:* Completely repainted by Kirkness and Innes, Eskbank, near Dalkeith in May 1968, "AVENGER" was photographed on the East Coast Night Trunk standing on the Royal Border Bridge at Berwick-upon-Tweed.   The roof tops of Berwick can be seen behind the Dress Macpherson tartaned Atkinson. Taken at half past nine at night at the end of a lovely sunny day in June 1968 and handled by one of the regular trunk drivers, Tam Inglis.

(photo Frank Richardson)

No. 51 THUNDERBIRD   *Above:*   A group of admirers chat to Charlie as he pulls out with the east coast night trunk.   Usually handled by an Atkinson, but in this case by "THUNDERBIRD" ERF Gardner 150.

(photo Frank Richardson)

No. 53 SILVER CLOUD   *Above:*   Charlie Waugh stands beside the AEC Mandator "SILVER CLOUD" in the car park of the Newcastle Arms, near Newark on Trent.   Tony the shunter has taken over the south bound trunk from Charlie at 6 a.m. at Newark, Charlie having driven down through the night from Musselburgh.   Tony has taken the trunk down to the night trunk depot at Nelson Street, Stepney, London, changed trailers and is back up to Newark about 5 p.m.   Charlie's regular digs were at the Newcastle Arms, North Muskham near Newark-on-Trent and having slept there during the day gets back into the vehicle about 5 o'clock at night and heads back north to Musselburgh.

(photo Frank Richardson)

No. 51 CARAVELLE

Left: Named after the French aeroplane No. 51 "CARAVELLE" heads back empty to Musselburgh. Photographed in Princes Street, Edinburgh the castle is in the background.
Behind the Atkinson are two Edinburgh Corporation Leyland double deckers.

(photo Frank Richardson)

No. 8 GIPSY MOTH

Right: Another vehicle which replaced an Albion Reiver was "GIPSY MOTH", and was named after the famous round the world yacht sailed by Sir Francis Chichester and was a Birmingham night trunk motor. Easily recognised by its blue and white Napier tartan sash, it is standing here in the Musselburgh yard on a Saturday morning.

(photo Frank Richardson)

No. 53 SILVER CLOUD   *Above:* Pollock's London Depot for the night trunk was located at EXPRESS CARRIERS LTD 42/52 Nelson Street, Stepney, London E1.   The entrance to this depot was quite narrow and "SILVER CLOUD" the AEC Mandator has made it round the back. Tony Mathews the Newark shunter is preparing to drop the Musselburgh trailer and prepare for the return trip back north.   The 1965 Mandator had received a new engine in June 1968.

(photo Frank Richardson)

No. 7 BURKE'S LAW   *Above:*   Named after the American TV series starring Gene Barry, this Atkinson Silver Knight was new in 1965. Here, it has just crossed over the bridge at Cockburnspath on the east coast main line heading south on the night trunk.   This photograph was taken at half past eight at night with Tam Inglis driving and you could almost set your watch by his regularity.

(photo Frank Richardson)

No. 7 BURKE'S LAW

Left: This shot was taken on the A1 south of Newark on Trent. The shunter, Tony Mathews has taken over the night trunk from the Scottish driver and is heading for the Stepney London depot. Taken early in the morning.   The Leyland Comet with the LAD cab belongs to the Danish Bacon Company.

(photo Frank Richardson)

No.7 BURKE'S LAW

Right: Heading north with the returning east coast night trunk, Tony Mathews the shunter, stops at a phone box to call the Musselburgh office for instructions. This was the normal means of communication before the mobile phone took over. "BURKE'S LAW" seen here is returning with the north bound night trunk trailer.   Night trunk units clocked up large weekly mileages between Musselburgh and London and although rarely seen as they ran through the night they were still kept in a clean condition.

(photo Frank Richardson)

No. 50 EARLYBIRD   *Above:* Tam Marshall was a farm lad from East Lothian and had recently joined Pollock prior to this photo taken in June 1968.   Tam was a tall lad standing over six feet and drove for Pollock until the end of 2006.   Farm lads took to articulated vehicles quite easily as growing up on farms they regularly handled tractors and trailers.

(photo Frank Richardson)

No. 29 FOUR SEASONS
Above: This 1966 Atkinson Silver Knight with Gardner 150 power has stopped on the Royal Border Bridge at Berwick-upon-Tweed when running south on the east coast night trunk.   Its just after 9 o'clock on a Saturday night in June 1968.   The width of the bridge has been reduced considerably since this photo was taken.

(photo Frank Richardson)

No. 37 COUNT DOWN

Above: The east coast night trunk ran down the A1 from Musselburgh to Stepney, London. The whole trip took about sixteen hours using two drivers. One of a pair of Rolls Royce powered Atkinson tractors bought new in 1969 "COUNT DOWN" was the last four wheel Atkinson tractor with the MK1 cab to join the fleet. The driver standing at the side is Tam Inglis who had come down to Pollock via the takeover of Dalkeith Transport and Storage. Eventually sold to Bernard Hunter, Edinburgh, crane hire specialists.

(photo Frank Richardson)

No. 41 GREAT SCOT   *Above:* The night trunk service required reliable vehicles to maintain regular deliveries.   New vehicles are an obvious answer and many found their way onto this service.   Here, "GREAT SCOT" the first Atkinson with a MKII cab to join the fleet stands whilst Charlie Waugh sen. checks the tyres on the trailer.   The cut away in the bumper gave a long appearance to the radiator.   This style didn't last long, being replaced on future Atkinsons with full bumpers.   Old style mirrors fitted.

(photo Frank Richardson)

No. 37 COUNTDOWN & No. 41 GREAT SCOT

Left and Below: These two views of Silver Knight Atkinson tractors taken in the same lay-by show the differences between the MK1 and MKII cabs. "COUNTDOWN" has one of the last MK1 cabs and "GREAT SCOT" the new MKII cab. Around this time the style of lettering on the doors was changed to throw the black shadow below the letters from the previous style of it being on top.

(photo Frank Richardson)

No. 1 APOLLO SEVEN

Opposite Page: This was a beautifully turned out Atkinson when new in October 1968. A local freelance artist, Sandy Maxwell usually painted the tartan sash and name. In some, but not all cases, the name of the tartan and date of painting were added in small letters within the tartan sash on the doors. One of the tricks of the trade when painting the tartans was to apply paint using the edges of small pieces of cardboard dipped in the paint.   The date on this vehicle was 22.10.68. This picture is included in the night trunk section because it spent most of its life at Express Carriers Depot in Nelson Street, Stepney, London. It must have had a hard life in London judging by the state of it, shown here in the yard at Musselburgh, some years later.   After service with Pollock it was seen in Tyson H Burridge colours.

(photo Frank Richardson)

No. 18 ROYAL SCOT

Left: Ian Pollock and driver Tam Liddle thought up the idea of the white roof and this was the first Atkinson if not the first vehicle in the fleet to which it was applied. "ROYAL SCOT" went on to the east coast night trunk when delivered new. Seen here in the yard at 101 Newbigging, Musselburgh in September 1969.

(photo Frank Richardson)

No. 2 ATKINSON BORDERER

Right: Driver Des Eccles photographed his Atkinson Borderer at Sydney Street, in London. This vehicle was stolen and never recovered. The livery on the Atkinson is considerably plainer than the previous Express MK I Atkinson tractor "APOLLO SEVEN".

(photo Des Eccles)

13

TANKERS

No. 15 FUGITIVE

Left: Although the Atkinson is shown here connected to the fuel tank trailer "FUGITIVE" was nearly always seen on ordinary trailer work.   Parked here in the Musselburgh yard.

(photo Frank Richardson)

No. 30 EARLY BIRD

Right: Rear view of fuel tank trailer connected to Atkinson "EARLY BIRD".   Parked in High Riggs at Tollcross, Edinburgh.

(photo Frank Richardson)

No. 50 EARLY BIRD

Above: "EARLY BIRD" was No. 50 in the fleet at this point and is parked at High Riggs in the Tollcross area of Edinburgh. The large building behind the vehicle is Goldbergs department store and the top of Edinburgh Castle can be seen in the distance. The Albion badge above the letter A on the radiator came from a Reiver.

(photo Frank Richardson)

No. 2 EURO SCOT

Above: Seen here in the Musselburgh yard in the colours of Shaws Fuels, this Atkinson tractor was eventually painted into Pollock's colours and given the name "EURO SCOT". The future direction of the fleet can be seen by the Scania parked behind.

(photo Frank Richardson)

No. 30 DAWN PATROL

Opposite Page: This Silver Knight Atkinson was one of the few equipped to handle fuel tanks. Standing just down the road from the yard at 101 Newbigging, Musselburgh, this shot shows the bright yellow instrument binnacles behind the windscreen. The passenger side binnacle was purely a dummy and from all accounts its only purpose was to present a balanced view of the vehicle.

(photo Frank Richardson)

No. 65 ROYAL SCOT

Below: Another 4x2 Atkinson with Gardner 180 power was VSC 333J. Sandwiched between trailers in the Musselburgh yard, it is in the dark blue colours of Shaws Fuels. Later when it was painted into Pollock's colours it was given the name "ROYAL SCOT".

(photo Frank Richardson)

No. 48 GEMINI II

Above: Delivered in 1966 this Atkinson eight wheeler was fitted with the fuel tank from No. 32 "PONDEROSA". It is standing in High Riggs, Tollcross, Edinburgh about 6 o'clock at night. Directly behind the tanker is Goldbergs department store and further back Edinburgh Castle can be glimpsed.

(photo Frank Richardson)

No. 61 FIERY SCOT
Left: This Atkinson six wheel rear-a-steer tractor started out on the heavy fuel oil tanker trailer and was usually driven by another of Pollock's gentlemen drivers, Dick Murray. Dick had been with Pollock almost from the very start and is seen here heading east along Bernard Street in Leith probably heading for Cockenzie Power Station.

(photo Joe Donaldson)

No. 6 FREE SCOT
Below Left and Right: This Atkinson tractor in Shaws Fuels colours was run by Pollock to deliver heavy fuel oil to local hospitals, power stations and factories. The Volvo F88 behind the tanker belonged to Donald Brown of Haddington. When the contract ended No. 6 was repainted into Pollock's colours and became "FREE SCOT".

(photos Frank Richardson)

14

SELECTION
OF FRONTS

Left: No. 3 TWO CAPITALS

Previous Page : No. 23 HIGH CHAPARRAL

Right: No. 45 PATHFINDER

No. 26 SCOTIA'S PRIDE

No. 46 TRIDENT II

No. 28 DAKTARI

No. 52 MIGHTY QUINN

15

GARAGE SHOTS

No. 33 DEFENDER

Above: By the time "DEFENDER" was in need of a repaint Pollock had their own painter called Jimmy Macarthur. He brush painted the cabs and also applied the tartan sash and names.   Before Jimmy the vehicles were painted mainly by Kirkness and Innes, Eskbank and a local freelance painter called Sandy Maxwell did the sash and names.   The tartan sash on this repaint contains the names EDINBURGH and GLASGOW as against the usual practice of EDINBURGH and LONDON. This came about as a result of the takeover by HTS who had an associate company called J & H Transport.   They had an office in Princess Docks, Glasgow which employed two men and was ran as a clearance house for return loads to the south.

(photo Frank Richardson)

No. 21 MOONSHOT   *Above:* This was the last AEC Marshal to enter service with Pollock.   This concluded a total of seven Ergomatic cab Marshals since the first one, "SCOTIA'S PRIDE" in 1967.   It's in the garage at Newbigging, Musselburgh for minor repairs.

(photo Frank Richardson)

No. 34 APACHE

Left: One of the Park Royal cab AEC Mercury tractors standing in the garage at Musselburgh. No. 34 "APACHE" and showing the Sutherland tartan on the radiator grill.

(photo Frank Richardson)

YARD SHED

Right: Looking into the 101 Newbigging Garage. The small Bedford van on the right DSF 222C was painted yellow and the LV cab ERF is "BEACHCOMBER" with one of the Atkinson tractors behind.

(photo Frank Richardson)

No. 9 UNTOUCHABLE

Above: "UNTOUCHABLE" driver Wullie Grandison stands beside the Atkinson giving it a final polish inside the garage at Musselburgh. The eight wheel ERF behind him is No. 14 YWS 111. According to ex-Pollock driver Bob Lumsden, Wullie was never a tight loader and was easily recognised when coming up behind him by the flapping sheets on the trailer.

(photo Frank Richardson)

16

YARD SHOTS

AEC MERCURY

Left: The 1954 MK I AEC Mercury is standing loaded outside the garage at 101, Newbigging, Musselburgh in the late 1950's. The man on the left was Monty Liddle brother-in-law of W G D Pollock. Next to him is the secretary Margaret Aitken and Miss Gibb who ran the office which at that time was situated at the entrance to the yard. On the extreme right is Sandy MacCormack the depot manager. Sandy had been depot manager with a local haulage contractor J Arnott at Wallyford and worked under WGD Pollock during nationalization.

(photo Pollock Collection)

ERF C15

Right: This early ERF tractor which was painted dark green lay at the back of the yard during the 1960's at Musselburgh. Both the chassis and cab were in very good condition with no sign of rust and would have made an excellent subject for restoration.

(photo Frank Richardson)

No.14 ERF
Above: The eight wheel ERF stands beside the fuel point at Newbigging, Musselburgh after finishing loading on a Saturday morning.

(photo Frank Richardson)

YARD SCENE

Left: This early 1960's photograph taken in the Newbigging yard shows the eight wheeler No. 14 YWS 111. Behind it is one of the four wheel AEC Mercurys dating from the mid 50's and away at the back is another AEC Mercury in the colours of William Watt. Its driver Jimmy Alves got regular work from Pollock, local and Glasgow loads. Buildings in the background on the other side of the street from the yard were demolished and a new fire station was built on the site.

(photo Pollock Collection)

No. 14 ERF

Right: Matty Kennedy spent most of his working life with Pollock and carried on well after retirement age. One of his first vehicles was the KV cab eight wheeler ERF No. 14. It's standing in the Musselburgh yard in the early 1960's with new tarpaulin and sheet whilst new housing is being built behind it. Pollock sold this land to the local council with the condition that a house would be allocated for the depot manager.

(photo Pollock Collection)

No. 8 ALBION REIVER

Left: Drivers Alec Fairbairn and Tam Liddle stand in front of the brand new Albion Reiver No. 8 outside the garage door in Musselburgh. Another driver Geordie Dunn was given it to drive. The building on the left was demolished in the early 1960's to allow greater space for the artics to manoeuvre. One of its unusual uses was to store pigs during a swine fever outbreak.

(photo Pollock Collection)

No. 8 ALBION REIVER

Right: The Albion Reiver is standing in the Newbigging yard and its fresh look suggests the photo was taken not long after its appearance at the Kelvin Hall Motor Show in Glasgow. This was always held in November and would date this to late 1961 or early 1962. The only Reiver to have a chrome bumper and chrome straps on the fuel tank.

(photo Pollock Collection)

YARD SHOT AEC. BEDFORD

Above: Transferring loads on a Saturday morning. The Bedford TK was used on local work. The AEC Marshal behind has an earlier Park Royal cab with two piece windscreen. The young driver in the centre is George MacLeod and the driver on the right is Jock Wilson. The pantiled building at the back was a joiner's business called James Leishman.

(photo Frank Richardson)

No. 12 GLOBE TROTTER

Above: "GLOBE TROTTER" loaded and standing in the yard.

(photo Frank Richardson)

No. 50 SCOTIA'S PRIDE

Left: This AEC Mandator was bought for the steel traffic to Birmingham and had a short life with the fleet.   Seen here in the Musselburgh yard between two Albion Reivers.

(photo Joe Donaldson)

No. 35 CANNONBALL

Right: This Atkinson's early years with Pollock were spent on the Birmingham night trunk and it was on this service that it crashed.   After repairs it returned to fleet service in October 1967 when this shot was taken.   Geordie Menzies the Musselburgh shunter is standing by on the forklift as "CANNONBALL" has just backed up on to a trailer on a typical dull dreich autumn day in the east of Scotland.

(photo Frank Richardson)

No. 52 THUNDERBIRD
Above: After the damage caused by the crash in October 1966 "THUNDERBIRD" was repaired and handed to another driver. Bob Cowe has the door open and is transferring his bits and pieces at the Musselburgh garage as the driver of "OVERLANDER" Matty Kennedy looks on.

(photo Frank Richardson)

No. 39 CRUSADER
Above: The Musselburgh shunters, Archie Shearer and Geordie Menzies check over the 1965 AEC Mercury "CRUSADER" as it stands outside the Musselburgh garage after a full repaint. Archie took over this vehicle after its repaint and it was used to gather local loads.

(photo Frank Richardson)

No. 54 MORRIS LD

Left: This van delivered small parcels locally in Musselburgh and Edinburgh areas and was also used as an introductory vehicle for young drivers entering the haulage industry.

(photo Frank Richardson)

No. 50 EARLY BIRD & No. 35 CANNONBALL

Right: Although the Atkinson on the left here "EARLY BIRD" is the newer of the pair it is the one on the right "CANNONBALL", a 1964 Gardner 150 powered tractor which has a fibreglass dummy radiator which later became standard on the MK II cabs in 1968.

(photo Frank Richardson)

AEC MARSHAL

Left: New AEC Marshal chassis standing in the yard at Musselburgh. Chassis No. 980 was one of a pair delivered in August 1968 the other Chassis No. being 1907. The spare wheel position was changed on these vehicles to fit centrally under the rear of the chassis.

(photo Frank Richardson)

No.38 WAYFARER & No. 40 VIRGINIAN

Right: Mechanic Bobby Vass chats to driver Wattie Howden as he transfers his gear to the brand new AEC Ergomatic cab Mercury "VIRGINIAN" LSC 100F. His old vehicle "WAYFARER" is on the left with headlight problems. February 1968.

(photo Frank Richardson)

No. 33 DEFENDER
Above: One of the last two Atkinson eight wheelers to be delivered to Pollock, "DEFENDER" was given to Jock Wilson.

(photo Frank Richardson)

No. 9 UNTOUCHABLE

Above: There was an American TV Cop series called The Untouchables running at this time on British TV.   Here, "UNTOUCHABLE" has been washed and is standing beside the fuel point.   The wheels are slightly turned out, showing the rear-a-steer arrangement.

(photo Frank Richardson)

No. 52 MIGHTY QUINN

Above: Wullie Grandison the driver of "Untouchable" in the yellow oilskin apron and a young Tam Marshall walk past the new arrival No. 52 "MIGHTY QUINN" with a new York tri-axle trailer and new tarpaulin, ropes and sheet. This was its very first load on Saturday 2nd March 1968 and it headed south to England the following day with Andrew Mack as its driver.

(photo Frank Richardson)

No. 28 DAKTARI   *Above:*   Having just completed loading on a Saturday morning, Alec Fairbairn gets ready to move the AEC and get the load covered in February 1968.   This particular load had over sixty different drops, mainly in the south of England.   Directly behind the headboard are cartons and drums of paint from Craig & Rose, Leith.   Above these are packages of stationery from Inveresk and away at the back are packages of books from Hunter & Foulis. Much has been written about the quality of AEC's at this time and there may be some truth here as this 1967 Marshal was re-engined in May 1968.

(photo Frank Richardson)

No. 28 DAKTARI

Left: Driver Alec Fairbairn is getting ready to cover the load on AEC Marshal "DAKTARI". Next in line is AEC Mercury No.47 "CARAVELLE" then another older AEC Mercury No.34 "APACHE". The unknown Atkinson tractor has just pulled into the Musselburgh yard on a Saturday morning in February 1968.

(photo Frank Richardson)

No. 20 POP NORTH

Right: This ergomatic cab AEC Marshal replaced the earlier 1961 Marshal called "FLYING SCOTSMAN" in 1968. Photographed in the Musselburgh yard in 1969.

(photo Frank Richardson)

No.40 VIRGINIAN and No. 31 BONANZA

Left: A rather sorry looking "BONANZA" is parked beside the AEC Mercury "VIRGINIAN" at Musselburgh. The Atkinson had returned from a spell working from the London depot. New in 1963 it was sold shortly after this picture was taken in 1968.

(photo Frank Richardson)

BENTLEY

Right: W G D Pollock's Bentley stands in front of the two AEC's "DAKTARI" and "CARAVELLE".

(photo Frank Richardson)

No. 23 HIGH CHAPARRAL   *Above:*   This Ergomatic cab AEC Marshal was named after the western TV series and was delivered in 1968. Its regular driver was Davy Scott whose previous vehicle was eight wheeler "TELSTAR" 888 SC.

(photo Frank Richardson)

No. 4 ALBION REIVER
Above: By 1968 most of the Albion Reivers had gone but No. 4 was receiving attention here in May 1968 with a view to putting it back on the road.

(photo Frank Richardson)

No. 62 BRAVE SCOT
Above: This Atkinson was one of three tractors which arrived along with a Guy Big J 4x2 tractor from the London firm George Transport from Hackney. They arrived at Musselburgh in the blue colours of Hilton Transport Services.

(photo Frank Richardson)

No. 22 STAR SCOT

Above: This 4x2 Atkinson tractor is seen here at Musselburgh and in fleet number terms replaced the eight wheel KV cab ERF VWS 200. When new it hauled a tank trailer.

(photo Frank Richardson)

YARD SCENE *Above:* Saturday mornings in the 1960's in the Newbigging yard were a scene of organised chaos. Lorries and trailers were being loaded and unloaded, vehicles were getting ready for a morning departure as well as those which were being loaded for leaving on the Sunday morning. Here the AEC Marshal "THE TALISMAN" is sandwiched between two of the Atkinson Silver Knights and boxed in at the back by an eight wheeler.

(photo Frank Richardson)

17

SCANIA

No 5. STOCKHOLMER

Above:- The first Scania appeared in the fleet in 1968 and was an LB110 tractor. Matty Kennedy was its first driver and is seen here in London.

(photo Arthur Ingram / Roundoak Publishing)

No. 24 LOWLAND SCOT

Above: The 1971 intake of new vehicles was a mixture of Scania LB 110's and Atkinson Borderers.   Lowland Scot was one of the Scanias and is standing in the June sunshine at the Musselburgh yard.

(photo Joe Donaldson)

No. 10 AMAZING GRACE

Above Right: One of the smaller LB 80 Scanias coupled to the Crane Fruehauf van "AMAZING GRACE" is parked here next to one of the Ex George Transport Atkinson Borderers, "BRAVE SCOT" at Musselburgh.

(photo Joe Donaldson)

No. 11 LOTHIAN SCOT

Right: Parked beside the fuel point in Musselburgh is another example of a Scania LB 110 tractor new in 1971.

(photo Joe Donaldson)

No. 39 AQUARIUS

Left: The small Scania arrived in 1969 in LB 80 form. Here Wattie Howden is filling up at the fuel pump in the Newbigging yard at Musselburgh.

(photo Joe Donaldson)

No. 51 MAJESTIC SCOT

Right: An electrical transformer forms part of the load behind one of the Scania LB 110 tractors which was bought new in 1970.

(photo Joe Donaldson)

18

ACCIDENTS

No. 52 THUNDERBIRD   *Page Opposite and this Page:*
On 1st October 1966 the ERF "THUNDERBIRD" was badly damaged in an accident on the A1.   It was returning home from the south, when the driver Tam Cleghorn had to take avoiding action and left the road.   Plunging down a 15 foot embankment he managed to keep the whole unit upright and stopped just short of the east coast main railway line.   As can be seen by the backward angle of the cab, serious damage was done to the chassis.   The local ERF agent Bowen repaired it but remained out of service until March 1967.   Prior to the accident it carried Fleet No. 52 but after repair and repaint it became No. 51.

(photos Frank Richardson)

MOBY DICK

Above: Wrecking and recovery tasks were no problem for this 4x4 AEC Matador named "MOBY DICK". It was sold to Fred McCabe who had a garage in Rosewell. Fred himself drove an AEC Marshal and was one of Pollock's sub-contractors. Jock Wilson stands in front here with his grandson standing on the tow bracket.

(photo Frank Richardson)

No.43 ROB ROY

Above: "ROB ROY" the AEC Mercury tractor arrived back in the yard at Musselburgh in March 1968 after jack-knifing in London. Although damaged it was still required to bring a loaded trailer back.

(photo Frank Richardson)

No. 51 CARAVELLE

Left: Rear view of the remains of "CARAVELLE" lying in the Musselburgh yard. This 1964 Atkinson Silver Knight was coming north on the return leg of the Birmingham night trunk when it struck a stationary vehicle near Moffat, Southern Scotland. It went on fire and as this photograph shows, it became a total wreck. This happened about November 1967.

(photo Frank Richardson)

ALBION REIVER

Right: A young Ian Pollock in the light coloured jacket and driver Matty Kennedy are amongst the group of people looking on at the front of the Reiver in the 1960's. It had come to grief as it returned from Penicuik, Midlothian with a load of paper from Cowans Paper Mill.

(photo Pollock Collection)

No.32 PONDEROSA

I photographed "PONDEROSA" in the garage at Musselburgh on Saturday 7th December 1968. I went there to get a lift home from Jock Wilson, (driver of "DEFENDER"). He said that the eight wheeler which was being driven south by Geordie Blair and loaded with paper from Galloway's Mill in Balerno had crashed into a tree at the Devils Beef Tub, Near Moffat. I took these without a flash at 1/30 sec, hence the poor quality. No 32 was written off and replaced with Atkinson artic "HIGHLAND WEDDING".

(photo Frank Richardson)

19

MISCELLANEOUS

No. 14 ERF

Left: Ex -Pollock No. 14 YWS 111 has been preserved by Willie Robson at his Honey Farm at Horncliffe just outside Berwick upon Tweed. It's on show here at the Biggar Rally in August 2005. The chassis of another ERF, a six wheeler, forms the load and hopefully another preservation project.

(photo Frank Richardson)

No. 1   BORDER LASSIE

Right: This ex–Pollock Atkinson Borderer has survived into preservation and at the time of this photograph it was owned by John Whinham from Wooler. It was called "BORDER LASSIE" and has a Berwickshire number plate. It was bought by Pollock along with another vehicle from a Scottish Border farmer called Aitken Young . It was never actually painted in the turquoise and red but in the brown and red which can be seen in the Atkinson tractor section of this book.   Parked on the grass here at the annual Vintage Vehicle Rally held at Biggar in August. John sold it on to Spence Haulage but it has since been sold back to Pollock in 2007.

(photo Frank Richardson)

No. 66 BRAW SCOT

Left: The Atkinson Borderer which is now shown at transport rallies is shown here in the original condition when bought by Scott Pollock from Alexander Reid, of Insch before any restoration was carried out.

(photo Pollock Collection)

No. 66 BRAW SCOT

Below: No. 66 was bought by Scott Pollock from a north of Scotland haulage contractor, Reid of Insch and purely intended as an entrant to the many vintage vehicle rallies which are held during the summer. It never actually saw service as a haulage vehicle with Pollock.   The previous "BRAW SCOT" was a Gardner 240 engined Atkinson 4x2 Borderer tractor. The show "BRAW SCOT" is standing in this shot at a transport gathering near the sea at Crammond, Edinburgh.

(photo Frank Richardson)

No. 3   TWO CAPITALS

Previous Page: The restored, "TWO CAPITALS" is seen at Gypsies Green stadium in South Shields at the end of the Tyne-Tees Rally.   Its owner was John Douglas and is a well known figure in the vintage vehicle rally scene and has restored a number of lorries. At the present time in 2007 it has been bought by Pollock who will continue to show it at Transport Rallies.

(photo Frank Richardson)

SCOTIAS PRYDE

Above: Jimmy Aitken, one of Pollock's maintenance team decided to try his hand at an owner driver. He bought this Dodge K series tipper brand new and named it "SCOTIAS PRYDE" on a MacLeod tartan sash. Photographed in the yard at Musselburgh after delivery from the paint shop.

(photo Frank Richardson)

B COWE

Left: Bob Cowe from Haddington was a Pollock's driver during the 1960's and after leaving became an HGV driving instructor at Motec Livingston. Eventually he set up his own HGV driver training company and also gave advice to companies and local authorities on training, regulations and Health and Safety issues. Always interested in transport and haulage Bob bought this AEC Mercury which had been new to Federation Breweries and rallied it during the summer months. This particular show was at Lennoxlove House near Haddington, home of the Duke of Hamilton. Sadly Bob is no longer with us as he died in October 1999.

(photo Frank Richardson)

SANDY SCOTT

Right: By all accounts this eight wheel Atkinson standing at the Bus Museum at Lathalmond in Fife in 2006 is ex-Pollock No. 24 "TELSTAR". Its original number plate 888 SC was retained by a previous owner.

(photo Frank Richardson)

No. 66 BRAW SCOT & No. 33 DEFENDER

Above: The livery style on the show vehicle "BRAW SCOT" hasn't changed much in the twenty years apart that these photographs were taken.
No. 33 "DEFENDER" is standing at the bus stop at Thorntonloch, East Lothian where the field over in the background is where Torness Power
Station would be built.

(photos Frank Richardson)

20

FLEET LIST

POLLOCK (Scotrans) Ltd
History:

W.G. D. Pollock (1935-1954)
Pollock (Musselburgh) Ltd (1954-1971)
H.T.S.(1971-1975)

Pollock (Musselburgh) Ltd
101 Newbigging
Musselburgh (1954-1981)
Pollock (Scotrans) Ltd
Olivebank
Musselburgh (1981-2006)

London Depots:-
Pollock (Musselburgh) Ltd
59 Hermitage Wall, Wapping
London E1

Incorporating:-

Daniel Forrest (approx. 1947)
Express Carriers (1957) (Joint Partner)
Dalkeith Transport (1963)
Alex C Walker (1969)
R S Pirnie (1976)

Stebondale Street
Isle of Dogs
London

Express Carriers Ltd
42/52 Nelson Street
Stepney, London E1

Coatbridge Depot:-
Palacecraig Street

Midlands Depot:-
Pensnett Estate
Kingswinford

Ft No.	Name	Reg No.	Year	Make	Tartan	Comments
		OTN 924		AEC Mammoth Major	None	Newcastle Registration
6		SH 8382		Leyland Steer	None	Berwickshire Registration
10		BKS 615		ERF 4 Wh flatbed	None	
		DHO 633		AEC	None	
		DPR 338		AEC Monarch	None	New to Drake
		DWS 382		ERF C15 Tractor	None	Pollock Transport on headboard
		DSG 886	1944	Leyland Beaver 4 Wh flatbed	None	Ex R M Pettigrew of Corstorphine
36	Crusader	DSY 971		ERF flatbed	None	
		ESF 888		ERF 6 Wh flatbed	None	
2		EVA 487		Leyland Beaver 4 Wh flatbed	None	Ex Scotts of Biggar
		EWS 353	1947	AEC 4 Wh Flatbed	None	Ex R M Pettigrew of Corstorphine
11		FFS 999		ERF 6 Wh flatbed	None	
		FSF 80/81?		Maudsley Mogul 4 Wh flatbed	None	Ex R M Pettigrew of Corstorphine
7		FSG 836	1947	Leyland Steer 6 Wh flatbed	None	Dan Forrest lettering on cab
32	Honest Lad	FSY 687		Leyland Octopus flatbed	None	Ex Dalkeith Transport
		GSF 514	1947/48	Vulcan 4 Wh flatbed	None	
		GSF 746	1947/48	AEC Monarch MK III	None	Ex R M Pettigrew of Corstorphine
41	Flying Dutchman	GSY 16		Morris 4 Wh flatbed	None	Sold to R&J Strang,Chapelhall, Airdrie
42	Tornado	GSY 17		Morris 4 Wh Tipper	None	
43		GSY 906		Morris 4 Wh flatbed	None	Sold to R&J Strang, Chapelhall,Airdrie
18		GWS 818		ERF 8 Wh flatbed	None	BRS colours
15		HSC 711	1950	Leyland Steer flatbed	None	
30		HSY 157		Albion Reiver flatbed	None	Ex Dalkeith Transport
33	Honest Lass	HSY 439	1961-66	Leyland Octopus flatbed	None	Ex Dalkeith Transport
28		JSY 254	1961-67	Albion Reiver flatbed	None	Ex Dalkeith Transport

Ft No.	Name	Reg No.	Year	Make	Tartan	Comments
27		JSY 255	1961-66	Albion Reiver 6 Wh flatbed	None	Ex Dalkeith Transport
44		JSY 704	1962	Morris 4 Wh flatbed	Dress McLeod	
26		JSY 789	1962-67	Albion Reiver 6 Wh flatbed	None	
16		JFG 275		Leyland Beaver 4 Wh flatbed	None	Ex Crawford, Fruit & Veg Merchant
		MSC 137	1954	AEC Mercury MKI 4 Wh flatbed	None	
		MSF 860	1955	AEC Mercury MKI 4 Wh flatbed	None	
		PSC 500	1957	Leyland Octopus flatbed	None	
		RSC 919	1958	ERF 6 Wh twin steer flatbed	None	Sold to Jack Smith, Wetherby
		RSG 930	1958	Leyland Octopus 8 Wh flatbed	None	
		TWS 200	1959	Leyland Comet 6 Wh flatbed	None	
				Commer 6 Wh flatbed	None	Write off accident south of Newark
5		UWS 200	1960	Leyland Octopus 8 Wh flatbed	None	
		VFS 20	1960	Leyland Steer 6 Wh flatbed	None	
22		VWS 200	1960	ERF KV 8 Wh flatbed	None	
46		WFS 320	1960-68	Leyland Comet 4 Wh flatbed	None	
23		WFS 350	1960-68	ERF KV 8 Wh flatbed	None	Destroyed by fire in Kent
19		WWS 310	1961	Albion Reiver 6 Wh flatbed	None	
2		XSF 400	1961	Albion Reiver 6 Wh flatbed	None	
21		YSC 300	1961-67	Albion Reiver 6 Wh flatbed	None	
14		YWS 111	1962	ERF KV8 Wh flatbed	None	Preserved by W Robson, Horncliffe
8		YWS 121	1962-67	Albion Reiver 6 Wh flatbed	None	
4		YWS 450	1963-67	Albion Reiver 6 Wh flatbed	None	
20	Flying Scotsman	YSC 888	1961-68	AEC Marshal 6 Wh flatbed	Brodie	
16	The Talisman	2640 SF	1962-68	AEC Marshal 6 Wh flatbed	Buchanan	
5	The Clansman	8555 SF	1963	AEC Marshal 6 Wh flatbed	Dress Stuart	

Ft No.	Name	Reg No.	Year	Make	Tartan	Comments
11	Night Scotsman	9797 SF	1963	Atkinson 8 Wh flatbed	Colquhoun	Sold to J Barrett
12	Globetrotter	33 SC	1963	Atkinson 8 Wh flatbed	Ogilvie	Sold to Crows
24	Telstar	888 SC	1963	Atkinson 8 Wh flatbed	None	Sold to Crows. Preserved
39		3720 SC	1963-68	Morris 4 Wh tractor	None	
40		3721 SC	1963-68	Morris 4 Wh tractor	None	
3	Two Capitals	3722 SC	1963	Atkinson 8 Wh flatbed	Innes	Sold to Crows. Back to Pollocks 2007
31	Bonanza	6030 SC	1963	Atkinson 4 Wh tractor	McLeod	
48/32	Ponderosa	7081 SC	1963-68	Atkinson 8 Wh tanker/flatbed	Jacobite	Write off in accident 1968
25	Scarlet O'Hara	8767 SC	1963	Atkinson 4 Wh tractor	Anderson	Sold to Dean
17	Avenger	AFS 150B	1964	Atkinson 4 Wh tractor	Dress McPherson	Sold to Ian Craig, Condorrat
35	Cannonball	ASC 780B	1964	Atkinson 4 Wh tractor		
49	Dakotas	AWS 410B	1964	Atkinson 4 Wh tractor		
50	Scotias Pride	AWS 411B	1964	AEC Mandator MKV tractor	Hunting MacMillan	
52/51	Thunderbird	AWS 412B	1964	ERF LV 4 Wh tractor	Barclay	Sold to Direct Transport, Shildon
51	Caravelle	BFS 265B	1964-67	Atkinson 4 Wh tractor	MacMillan	Destroyed by fire 1967
53	Silver Cloud	BFS 266B	1964	AEC Mandator MKV tractor	MacBeth	
36	Beachcomber	CSC 22B	1964	ERF LV 4 Wh tractor	MacPherson	
6	Goldfinger	CSC 33B	1964	Atkinson 4 Wh tractor	Lindsay	Sold to A Hewitt
1	Stingray	CSC 44B	1964 -66	AEC Mercury 4 Wh tractor	McLaren	
34	Apache	CSC 55B	1964	AEC Mercury 4 Wh tractor	Sutherland	Sold to Houston
39	Crusader	CSF 444C	1965	AEC Mercury 4 Wh tractor	Fraser	
7	Burke's Law	CWS 400C	1965	Atkinson 4 Wh tractor	Kennedy	Sold to Wright
43	Rob Roy	DFS 66C	1965	AEC Mercury 4 Wh tractor	MacGregor	
15	Fugitive	DFS 77C	1965	Atkinson 4 Wh tractor	42nd Black Watch	
		DSF 222C	1965	Bedford Van	Painted yellow	

Ft No.	Name	Reg No.	Year	Make	Tartan	Comments
37	Sundowner	DSF 700C	1965	AEC Mercury 4 Wh tractor	MacLean	
10	Shangri'la	DSC 11C	1965	Atkinson 4 Wh tractor	Clan Chatton	
30/50	Early Bird	ESF 404C	1965	Atkinson 4 Wh tractor	McLaren	
54		ESC 333C	1965-68	Morris LD Van		
45	Pathfinder	FFS 20D	1966	Bedford TK 4 Wh flatbed	Dress Stuart	
42	Trail Trekker	FFS 21D	1966	Bedford TK 4 Wh flatbed	Buchanan	
41	Moonspinner	FFS 22D	1966	AEC Mercury 4 Wh tractor	MacNab	
38	Wayfarer	FFS 23D	1966	AEC Mercury 4 Wh tractor	Baird	
1	Day Tripper	FFS 140D	1966	AEC Mercury 4 Wh tractor	McLeod of Lewis	
19	Overlander	FFS 800D	1966	Atkinson 4 Wh tractor	Campbell of Argyll	Sold to J Brown, Hamilton
29	Four Seasons	FFS 801D	1966	Atkinson 4 Wh tractor	Balmoral	
2	Pacemaker	FSG 450D	1966	Atkinson 4 Wh tractor	Cameron of Erracht	
33	Defender	HSF 12E	1967	Atkinson 8 Wh flatbed	Duncan	Sold to Jobling Purser
26	Scotia's Pride	JSG 606E	1967	AEC Marshal 6 Wh flatbed	Montgomery	
28	Daktari	JWS 999F	1967	AEC Marshal 6 Wh flatbed	Hunting MacIntyre	Sold to D D & L Finlayson, Broxburn
18	Gypsy Moth	JSC 555E	1967	Atkinson 4 Wh tractor	Napier	
30	Dawn Patrol	JSG 666E`	1967	Atkinson 4 Wh tractor		
9	Untouchable	KWS 666F	1967	Atkinson 6 Wh tractor	MacLaine of Lochbuie	Rear-a-steer
40	Virginian	LSC 100F	1968	AEC Mercury 4 Wh tractor	Menzies	Sold to Harry Oliver
47	Caravelle	LSC 6F	1968	AEC Mercury 4 Wh tractor	MacMillan	Awaiting restoration
52	Mighty Quinn	LSF 789F	1968	Leyland Beaver 4 Wh tractor	Ancient MacMillan	
		LSG 66F	1968	Bedford Van		
23	High Chaparral	LSG 111F	1968	AEC Marshal 6 Wh flatbed	Hunting MacPherson	Sold to J M K Ireland
31	Bonanza	NFS 44G	1968	Atkinson 4 Wh tractor	Dress McLeod	

Ft No.	Name	Reg No.	Year	Make	Tartan	Comments
16	Lively Lady	NFS 4G	1968	AEC Marshal 6 Wh flatbed	Chisholm	
20	Pop North	NFS 55G	1968	AEC Marshal 6 Wh flatbed	Buchanan	
46	Trident II	NFS 88G	1968	AEC Mercury 4 Wh flatbed	Skene	Sold to Thomas Stirling, Glasgow
1	Apollo Seven	NSF 120G	1968	Atkinson 4 Wh tractor	Dress Stewart	Express Carriers. Sold to T H Burridge
54		NSF 700G	1968	Commer Van		
4	Saturn V	NWS 600G	1968	AEC Marshal 6 Wh flatbed	Forbes	
56	Famous Scot	NSC 877G	1968	Albion Clydesdale 4 Wh flatbed	Livingstone	Ex Alex C Walker. Sold to James Holmes
55	Star Trek	NFS 80G	1968	Albion Clydesdale 4 Wh flatbed	Erskine	Ex Alex C Walker. Sold to HTS Gateshead
21	Moonshot	NWS 888G	1968	AEC Marshal 6 Wh flatbed	Mackenzie	
37	Count Down	OSG 21G	1968	Atkinson 4 Wh tractor		Sold to Bernard Hunter
41	Great Scot	OSG 700G	1968	Atkinson 4 Wh tractor	Farquharson	
5	Stockholmer	OWS 3G	1968	Scania LB110 4 Wh tractor	Kerr	
19	Dandy Scot	SSF 21H	1969	Atkinson 4 Wh tractor	MacRae	
44	Snoopy	PSG 600G	1968	AEC Mercury 4 Wh flatbed	Bruce	Sold to HTS Gateshead
65	Wild Scot	AGF 982G	1968	Guy Big J 4 Wh tractor	Shaw	Ex HTS. Sold to Baxter, Tranent
18	Royal Scot	PSG 11H	1969	Atkinson 4 Wh tractor	MacArthur	
42	Eagle	PSG 888H	1969	AEC Mercury 4 Wh flatbed	McLaughlan	Sold to HTS Charlton
45	Columbia	PWS 2H	1969	AEC Mercury 4 Wh flatbed	Chisholm	Sold to T Blaikie, Musselburgh
53	Regal Scot	RFS 777H	1969	Scania LB110 4 Wh tractor	Dress Stewart	
39	Aquarius	RWS 515H	1969	Scania LB80 4 Wh tractor	Royal Stewart	
	Bold Scot	RWS 636H	1969	Atkinson 4 Wh tractor	Murray of Atholl	Sold to Direct Transp, then Preistner
57	Odyssey	SSF 20H	1969	Scania LB80 4 Wh tractor	Napier	
19	Dandy Scot	SSF 21H	1969	Atkinson 4 Wh tractor	MacRae	
25	Supreme Scot	SSF 22H	1969	Scania LB80 4 Wh tractor	Buchanan	
58	Anglo Scot	TSC 500J	1970	Bedford CF Van	MacLaine of Lochbuie	

Ft No.	Name	Reg No.	Year	Make	Tartan	Comments
22	Star Scot	TSF 2J	1970	Atkinson 4 Wh tractor	McQueen	
61	Fiery Scot	USC 30J	1970	Atkinson 6 Wh tractor	Sinclair	
51/27	Majestic Scot	USF 700J	1970	Scania LB110 4 Wh tractor	Scot	
59	Noble Scot	UFS 22J	1970	ERF 4 Wh tractor	Leslie	Eventually painted into OCL colours
63/15	Rebel Scot	VSC 110J	1970	Scania LB110 4 Wh tractor	Innes	
65/9	Royal Scot	VSC 333J	1970	Atkinson 4 Wh tractor		Ex Shaws Fuels Colours
39	Gallant Scot	USF 555J	1970	Scania LB110 4 Wh tractor	Menzies	
9	Royal Scot	USC 333J	1970	Atkinson Borderer 4 Wh tractor	Dress MacPherson	
2	Brave Scot	FLO 968J	1970	Atkinson 4 Wh tractor	Morrison	Ex HTS
63	Swift Scot	FLO 969J	1970	Atkinson 4 Wh tractor	Hunting MacLean	Ex HTS
64	Gay Scot	FLO 970J	1970	Atkinson 4 Wh tractor	Ramsay	Ex HTS. Sold to Direct Transport
1	Fair Scot	VKG 732J	1970	Atkinson Borderer	MacLaine of Lochbuie	
24	Lowland Scot	WFS 800K	1971	Scania LB110 4 Wh tractor	MacGregor	
11	Lothian Scot	WFS 810K	1971	Scania LB110 4 Wh tractor	Hamilton	
36	Proud Scot	WFS 811K	1971	Atkinson Borderer 4 Wh tractor	Cunningham	Sold to Direct Transport
38	Able Scot	XFS 600K	1971	Atkinson Borderer 4 Wh tractor	Mackay	Sold to Direct Transport
1	Fair Scot	XSC 860K	1971	Atkinson Borderer 4 Wh tractor	MacIntosh	
37	Wise Scot	XSC 850K	1971	Atkinson Borderer 4 Wh tractor	Wallace	
7	Braw Scot	CSC 99L	1972	Atkinson Borderer 4 Wh tractor	Hutchison	Gardner 240
10	Amazing Grace	CSC 100L	1972	Scania LB80 4 Wh tractor	Johnstone	Sold to Peart Brothers
3	Drummer Boy	CSC 101L	1972	Scania LB80 4 Wh tractor	Davidson	
2		CSG 500L	1972	Atkinson Borderer 4 Wh tractor		Express Carriers
6	Free Scot	BFS 839L	1972	Atkinson Borderer 4 Wh tractor	MacNeil	Ex Shaws Fuels colours
18	Joe 90	RTF 899L	1972	Volvo F88 290 4 Wh tractor	Buchanan	
2	Euro Scot	AWS 770L	1972	Atkinson Borderer 4 Wh tractor	Shaw	Ex Shaws Fuels colours. Sold to Clark
1	Border Lassie	KSH 123L	1972	Atkinson Borderer 4 Wh tractor		Back in Pollock's ownership 2007